REMBRANDT

A Biography by ELIZABETH RIPLEY

Published by Oxford University Press

REMBRANDT

With Drawings, Etchings
and Paintings by Rembrandt

NEW YORK   HENRY Z. WALCK, INC., DISTRIBUTORS   1955

ILLUSTRATIONS

THREE HUNDRED FIFTY years ago in the town of Leyden in Holland lived a miller whose name was Harmen. Harmen van Rijn he was called, because his mill was on the River Rhine. He and his sons worked hard, and the mill prospered. In the year 1606 Harmen's fourth son was born and he was named Rembrandt van Rijn.

The little Rembrandt liked to play alone under the flickering light of the mill; but when he was seven years old, his father sent him to school. Although Rembrandt worked hard, books did not interest him. He preferred to climb to the loft of the mill with his younger sister and watch the quivering light play on her pretty face. He often drew pictures of her as she sat in the half-light of the mill loft. He loved to sketch windmills against cloudy skies and shadows moving across wide fields. He longed to become an artist, so that he could paint everything he saw. Harmen was proud of his son's drawings and he decided to send the boy to study with an artist named Swanenburg.

Rembrandt was seventeen when he entered Swanenburg's studio. There he learned how to mix paints and prepare canvases. He was taught to draw with a needle on a copper plate which could be used to print the same picture many times. The printed picture was called an etching.

For three years Rembrandt worked happily in Swanenburg's studio. Then one day the master told his quiet pupil that he had no more to teach him, so Rembrandt decided to go to Amsterdam to study with an artist named Lastman. But the noisy city frightened the shy miller's son, and soon he returned to the peaceful mill in Leyden.

Rembrandt set up an easel in his home and painted all day. Harmen, after he had worked hard at the mill, liked to sit while his son made etchings of his wrinkled face. It amused the miller to dress in the strange costumes Rembrandt had brought from Amsterdam. In one etching the old man wears a high turban and in another, a fur cap.

Rembrandt made so many etchings of his father that today many people are familiar with the face of the honest miller who lived more than three hundred years ago.

REMBRANDT'S FATHER   1630
Pierpont Morgan Library, New York

REMBRANDT'S FATHER   1630
Pierpont Morgan Library, New York

Early each morning Harmen and his three oldest sons went to work at the mill. Quiet settled over the van Rijn house. Rembrandt, painting in his studio, could hear the soft whir of his mother's spinning wheel, as she sat working by the window in the next room.

Rembrandt loved to draw his mother's gentle face. He drew her while she worked wearing a plain dark dress and a huge white bonnet. He never asked her to dress in strange costumes like those his father loved to wear.

Sometimes when she had finished her work she would open her heavy Bible, put her glasses on the end of her nose, and start to read. One day he painted her bending over the huge book. She wears a brown dress and a heavy velvet hood. The light which shines on the white pages of the book is reflected in her face. Her mouth is slightly open as she concentrates on her reading. This is only one of the many pictures Rembrandt painted of his mother. Hour after hour she would sit for him patiently, for she had a deep affection for her quiet artist son.

REMBRANDT'S MOTHER   1628
Pierpont Morgan Library, New York

REMBRANDT'S MOTHER   1628
Pierpont Morgan Library, New York

REMBRANDT'S MOTHER   1629
Wilton House, England

Many beggars roamed the countryside around Leyden when Rembrandt was living there. For years Holland had been fighting to free herself from the Spaniards, who had ruled her cruelly. After a long bloody war she had won her independence, but many people were hungry and homeless.

As Rembrandt wandered through the town, he saw haggard men and women dressed in rags, huddled around a small fire. He sketched one miserable old man as he sat warming his hands. A poor woman walked by with a bundle in her arms. Her back was bent from hard work. With a few simple strokes of his pen Rembrandt sketched her as she passed.

When he returned to his studio, he made etchings from his drawings. One shows a man with a bulbous nose and tattered clothes. He holds a knobby stick behind his back as if to balance his fat stomach which protrudes in front.

From Amsterdam came letters from friends, urging Rembrandt to come to the city and learn to draw in the style of the great Italian painters who had lived one hundred years before. But the miller's son was not interested in imitating those painters who drew beautifully proportioned nude figures in smooth, neat outlines. He believed that an artist should make pictures of the people he saw around him. So, over and over, he sketched real men and women dressed in rags, and from his sketches he made etchings of the wretched beggars of Leyden.

BEGGAR WARMING HIS HANDS   1630
Pierpont Morgan Library, New York

BEGGAR   1630
Pierpont Morgan Library, New York

BEGGAR WOMAN   1630
Pierpont Morgan Library, New York

Rembrandt looked at himself in the mirror. His blond curly hair stood out wildly from his head. Hunching up his shoulders, he let out a fierce shout. He studied his face intently to see how his eyebrows came together and his jaw pushed forward. The ferocious expression fascinated him and in quick rapid strokes he sketched what he saw.

In one year he made twenty etchings of his face. One shows him laughing; another, surprised. Art dealers from Amsterdam visited Rembrandt and were impressed with the young artist's portraits. More and more often they came to buy his etchings. Soon Rembrandt received orders from prosperous Dutch merchants who wanted him to come to Amsterdam to paint their portraits.

Rembrandt decided that he had lived in Leyden long enough. He was now twenty-six years old. His father had died, leaving the mill to his oldest sons, who had little in common with their artist brother. Only his good mother understood her quiet, hard-working son. Regretfully he said good-by to her. Then he packed his paints and canvases and set out for Amsterdam in search of success.

SELF PORTRAITS   1630
Pierpont Morgan Library, New York

Amsterdam was a prosperous city in 1632. Along her canals were many fine houses. One of them belonged to a well-known surgeon whose name was Tulp, because of the large tulip which was carved on the front of his house. Twice a week Dr. Tulp lectured on anatomy in the amphitheater of the college of surgeons. His students gathered around him while he skillfully dissected a body. In Rembrandt's day, anatomy lessons were so popular that fashionable men and women came to watch the demonstrations. Many doctors commissioned artists to paint pictures of them lecturing on anatomy.

Soon after Rembrandt arrived in Amsterdam, Dr. Tulp called at his studio. He wanted the young artist to paint a picture which would show him lecturing to seven members of the college of surgeons.

This was Rembrandt's first big order. On a canvas five feet by seven he had to include eight life-size figures and a corpse. Rembrandt did not want to copy the style of other artists of his day. Instead of placing the eight doctors in a row, he arranged the group of figures in the shape of a pyramid. A strong light shines on the table where the corpse is lying and plays on the faces of the eight doctors. Rembrandt painted the heads with great care in order that each should be a perfect likeness. Three of the doctors lean over the table, watching the demonstration with intense interest. Two stand at the near side of the table, their heads turned in profile. Another holds a paper on which are written the names of the eight surgeons. The only doctor who does not look at the corpse is the one whose head forms the top of the pyramid. To the right, behind the table, sits Dr. Tulp, dressed in a black cloak and broad-brimmed hat. Light shines on his face, his white starched collar, and his sensitive surgeon's hands.

Rembrandt was only twenty-six years old when he painted "The Anatomy Lesson." It was a daring experiment, but it was successful. Proudly Dr. Tulp and the seven surgeons hung the picture in their amphitheater. Suddenly the young artist from Leyden became a popular portrait painter in Amsterdam.

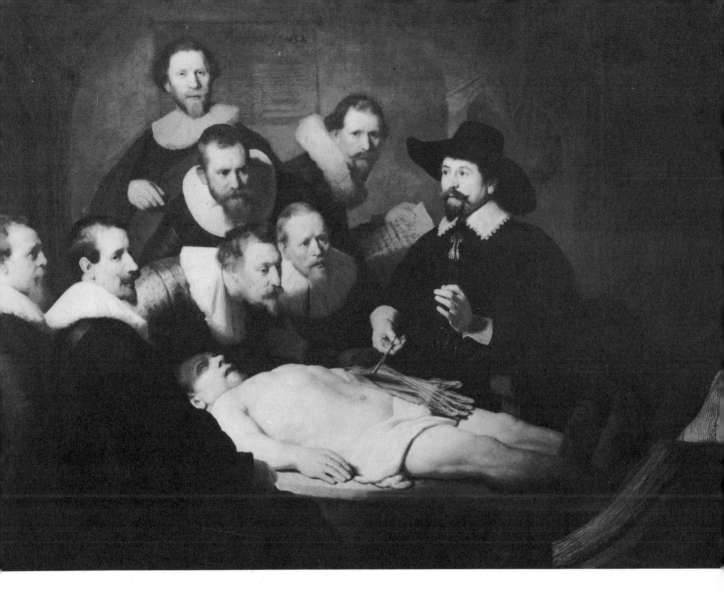

THE ANATOMY LESSON OF DR. TULP 1632
Mauritshuis, The Hague

Rembrandt rented a studio beside a canal in a quiet section of Amsterdam. Almost every day prosperous citizens came to his door asking him to paint their portraits. They did not expect the young artist to flatter them. They only asked to be painted as they were, austere in their black suits and broad-brimmed hats. Their wives, too, were severely clad in somber dresses and white caps. Rembrandt painted perfect likenesses of his clients, and because of the half-light which played on their humorless faces, they seemed alive.

When he had time Rembrandt painted pictures for his own amusement. He painted a picture of a philosopher sitting at his desk, deep in thought. The light from the window above his open book shines on his face and casts a bright spot on the floor behind him. The rest of the room is dark, but from the shadows emerges a winding staircase, which turns in a sweeping spiral and disappears into the darkness of the lofty ceiling. An arched door-way under the staircase leads to another mysteriously lighted room.

Constantly Rembrandt searched for light in deep shadow, and it is this subtle light which plays even in the darkest corners of his pictures.

THE PHILOSOPHER WITH OPEN BOOK   1633
Louvre, Paris

In two years Rembrandt had become the most popular portrait painter in Amsterdam. He was only twenty-eight years old. Order after order poured in, and he became rich. He loved to dress in splendid costumes. He bought plumed hats, embroidered cloaks, and pieces of antique armor. Once he painted a picture of himself, wearing a huge velvet beret and a collar of shining steel. The heavy velvet cloak which covers one shoulder is fastened at the neck by an elaborate gold chain.

This richly dressed young man gazes from the picture with an air of assurance, for the quiet miller's son from Leyden was now Holland's most successful portrait painter.

SELF PORTRAIT   1634
Kaiser-Friedrich Museum, Berlin

Saskia van Uylenburgh was the daughter of wealthy Dutch parents and the cousin of an art dealer in Amsterdam. Rembrandt met her when she called one day at her cousin's shop. He was instantly charmed by her fresh blond beauty. Her curly hair and pink cheeks reminded him of his little sister Elizabeth. When he met her again, he asked if he might paint her portrait. Happily Saskia agreed to sit for Amsterdam's most fashionable artist. His wavy hair, fine clothes, and gallant manner intrigued her, and she loved to dress in the fine costumes the artist kept in his studio. Many times Rembrandt painted her smiling young face, so different from the stern heavy faces of his clients. When one day he boldly asked her to marry him, Saskia van Uylenburgh consented.

A year passed before the couple were married, but during that year Rembrandt painted seven portraits of his pretty fiancée. One day she posed for him, wearing a purple velvet robe with light green sleeves and an elaborately embroidered collar. On her head is a huge hat lined with red velvet and trimmed with a white plume. Pearls decorate her wrists and neck, and a huge pearl dangles from her jeweled earring. In her delicate hand she holds a sprig of fresh rosemary, which in Rembrandt's day was the symbol for a young girl who is about to be married.

SASKIA   1634
Kassel, Germany

One bright July day in 1634, Rembrandt and Saskia were married. Proudly the artist took his wife to his house on Breedstraat (Broad Street) in Amsterdam. He bought her velvet robes, brocaded cloaks, and precious jewels. Dressed in magnificent finery, she sat for hours while her husband painted her.

When customers flocked to Rembrandt's studio, asking to have their portraits painted, he accepted every order; for he wanted money to buy beautiful costumes for Saskia and art treasures for his home. Fat Dutch merchants, wealthy bankers and their stylishly dressed wives posed in Rembrandt's studio.

One of Rembrandt's models was a fashionable gentleman, named Maerten Day, who had been an officer in the Dutch army. In his portrait he is elegantly dressed in a black-and-white striped suit trimmed with a wide lace collar and lace knee ruffles. His shoes are decorated with enormous lace rosettes. When the picture was finished, Rembrandt painted a portrait of Day's wife (Johanna Machteld Van Doorn) which shows her dressed in a gown of black brocaded silk trimmed with elaborate lace. In her hand she holds a fan of black ostrich feathers. The portraits were perfect likenesses and every detail was painted with great care. Maerten Day and his wife were delighted.

MAERTEN DAY   1634
Collection Baron Alain de Rothschild, Paris

JOHANNA VAN DOORN   1634
Collection Baron Alain de Rothschild, Paris

In his studio Rembrandt gave lessons to students who wanted to paint in the style of Amsterdam's most successful artist. Every day pupils and clients visited the house on Breedstraat. While Rembrandt taught and painted, Saskia moved quietly about the home.

In the evening after the last client had departed, Rembrandt put away his brushes and sat down to supper with his wife. One festive evening he put on a huge black hat with a sweeping plume and a coat of fiery red. Around his waist he buckled a huge sword with a jeweled handle. Saskia wore a dress of pale blue satin. On the table was a splendid pie, upon which sat a stuffed peacock.

Rembrandt watched the soft candlelight play on Saskia's smiling face. Then he took her on his knee and, holding his glass of amber-colored beer high in the air, drank a toast to his pretty wife.

Later, Rembrandt painted this gay scene. The red-coated cavalier is laughing as he offers a toast to the beautiful bride he holds proudly on his knee. It is the happiest picture Rembrandt ever painted.

REMBRANDT AND SASKIA 1634
Dresden Gallery, Germany, Photo Alinari

Rembrandt's house on Breedstraat was in the center of the Jewish quarter of Amsterdam. Rabbis and scholars visited the artist's studio. Their dark bearded faces interested Rembrandt far more than the heavy stolid faces of his wealthy clients. He made friends with the tradesmen who sold him bright-colored rugs and pieces of ancient armor. When he walked through the busy streets he talked with the poor people and studied their expressions. Some of them were his models for pictures of Bible stories, and he dressed them in oriental turbans and rich brocaded robes.

He painted a picture of Samson wearing a beautiful green and yellow coat and a jewel-handled sword at his hip. He is standing outside the home of his father-in-law, angrily demanding that he be allowed to see his bride. His thick wavy hair falls over his shoulders. Raising his fist in the air, he shakes it threateningly at the old man in a red skull cap who peers from a small window.

Over and over Rembrandt painted scenes from the life of Samson. He had read the stories often in his mother's big Bible, and he loved to tell them dramatically in his pictures.

SAMSON THREATENING HIS
FATHER-IN-LAW   1638
Kaiser-Friedrich Museum, Berlin

On a winter day in 1635 Rembrandt's and Saskia's first son was born, but he only lived a few days. Rembrandt was heartbroken.

A few months later he made a beautiful drawing of the Bible story of the return of the prodigal son, and it expressed with deep feeling the love of a father for his child. He etched the drawing on a copper plate and printed the picture many times. At last he had a print which satisfied him.

The picture shows the prodigal son, haggard and worn, kneeling at his father's feet, imploring forgiveness. He has spent his money recklessly and lost all his possessions. His only clothing is a cloth around his hips. His father has rushed out of doors to meet him, and tenderly bends over his penitent son. The servant who stands in the doorway holds a pair of shoes and a heavy robe. Another servant peers from the window above the father's head.

The gentle and understanding face of the father perhaps expresses Rembrandt's own feeling of sadness for the loss of his baby son.

THE PRODIGAL SON 1636
Pierpont Morgan Library, New York

Rembrandt always carried a sketchbook when he walked about Amsterdam, for he loved to take notes on the life he saw around him. The busy streets were filled with people from many countries, some of them dressed in strange costumes. He indicated a whole group of people with only a few simple lines, never cluttering his drawings with unnecessary details.

He loved to study the forms and movements of animals. When a traveling circus visited Amsterdam, he made several beautiful drawings of lions, and once he drew a picture of an elephant. With a few strokes of his bamboo pen he noted its heavy bulk and the thick folds of its skin. The great lumbering elephant seems very much alive.

ELEPHANT 1637
Albertina, Vienna

On warm summer days Rembrandt liked to walk out into the country. Sometimes Saskia went with him and sat beside him as he sketched. They loved the peace of the fields and the wide open sky. Rembrandt filled the pages of his sketchbook with pen-and-ink drawings of windmills and bridges. In a few strokes he noted the skyline of a village or the outline of a tree.

When he returned to his studio he put his carefully drawn studies aside and dreamed of landscapes he had never seen. He often painted high mountains, rocky cliffs, or towering castles. Even the bridges and rivers were not copies of the ones he had drawn so accurately in his sketchbook. In all of Rembrandt's landscape paintings the skies are dark and stormy, but in every one sunlight filters through the clouds, picking out the form of a tree or a figure and shining dramatically on the surface of shimmering water.

LANDSCAPE WITH STONE BRIDGE　1639
Rijksmuseum, Amsterdam

One winter day in 1639 Rembrandt and Saskia moved into a fine new home on Breedstraat, not far from where they had lived when they were first married. It was a handsome three-storied house with arched windows and stone carvings on the front. Rembrandt's studio was on the first floor. The second floor was divided into small studios so that each of his students could work undisturbed. In every room were carved cabinets in which Rembrandt kept the precious treasures he had collected. Rich tapestries and bright paintings hung on every wall.

Rembrandt and Saskia were happy in their new home, and hardly ever left it. Sometimes Rembrandt went to visit his aging mother in Leyden. He brought her fine clothes and expensive jewels, and once he painted a picture of her dressed in a brown velvet hood. Her fur-lined cloak is fastened by a huge jeweled clasp. Her wrinkled hands are resting on a cane. This was the last portrait Rembrandt painted of his mother, for she died the next year.

REMBRANDT'S MOTHER 1639
Vienna Gallery, Vienna

Titus van Rijn was born in the fall of 1641. This was a happy day for Saskia and Rembrandt. But Saskia was far from well, and Rembrandt watched anxiously by her bedside. Only when he shut himself in his studio was he able to forget his worries.

Captain Banning Cocq, commander of a regiment of civic guards, had commissioned Rembrandt to paint a life-size group portrait of his regiment. The idea appealed to Rembrandt, for he had often watched Dutch regiments preparing themselves for a march. Dressed in plumed hats and shining armor, each member came to pose in Rembrandt's studio and each contributed an equal amount of money to have his portrait painted.

Through the winter and spring Rembrandt worked on the huge canvas, while Saskia grew weaker. One June day she sent for a lawyer and asked him to draw up her will. Ten days later she died. She was only twenty-nine years old. Saskia was buried in the graveyard of West Church. Sadly Rembrandt returned to the quiet house on Breedstraat. Overwhelmed with loneliness, he shut himself in his studio and began once more to work on the picture of Captain Banning Cocq's regiment.

When the picture was finished the captain was very pleased. The tall black uniformed commander stands in the center of the canvas, giving orders to his lieutenant, who is dressed in yellow. A strong light shines on the two central figures, but most of the guardsmen are plunged in darkness. Rembrandt had inscribed their names on a shield in the upper part of the picture, but the other members of the regiment were far from satisfied. Some of the faces were almost hidden, and a small dog and a little girl dressed in yellow were more noticeable than the guardsmen themselves.

The painting hung in a dark corner of the Regiment Hall for many years. It became so blackened by tobacco smoke that people named it "The Night Watch." Today the guardsmen who complained so bitterly have been forgotten, but "The Night Watch" is one of the world's most famous paintings.

THE NIGHT WATCH   1642
Rijksmuseum, Amsterdam

Rembrandt's picture "The Night Watch" shocked the stolid citizens of Amsterdam. They did not realize that the painting was a masterpiece of glowing light in deep shadow. A group portrait, they believed, should show orderly rows of faces, evenly lighted. Even Captain Banning Cocq refused to defend the picture publicly. Rich merchants no longer clamored to have their portraits painted. Day after day went by, and no one called at the studio on Breedstraat.

The lonely Rembrandt had only his baby son Titus to keep him company. Sometimes in order to escape from the big house so full of memories of Saskia, he would take long walks through the city streets or along the canals of Amsterdam. He always carried a pen and sketchbook, and to his belt he fastened a flask of ink. With a few strokes of his pen he would indicate the silhouette of a house, the outline of a tree, or the shape of a bridge. He modeled the forms here and there with a transparent ink wash. The quick luminous studies helped him to store impressions in his mind. These impressions were the inspirations for his beautiful landscape etchings.

BRIDGE OF GRIMNSESSESLUIS, AMSTERDAM
Louvre, Paris

Rembrandt made an etching of three trees standing on a hill, dark against a vast sky. The picture was not a copy of one of his drawings. He imagined a landscape he had never seen, and he drew it in his studio, using a copper plate on which he had once etched some faces. The faint profiles may be seen in the light part of the sky.

The foreground of the picture is in deep shadow. Black streaks of rain darken the left part of the sky. But in the background the sun shines and the sky is bright. The tragedy and hope which Rembrandt saw in all nature is expressed in his beautiful etching "The Three Trees."

THE THREE TREES   1643
Pierpont Morgan Library, New York

Day after day Rembrandt worked alone in his studio, stopping only to eat the bread and herring which Titus' nurse brought him. He hardly talked to anyone, except to give instructions to the pupils who continued to come to him, hoping to learn his secret of painting light in shadow.

To comfort himself in his loneliness he painted several pictures of the Baby Jesus and his Mother Mary, which made him think of his own happy family life with Saskia. One picture shows a mother and child in a simple Dutch home. The mother, who has stopped reading her Bible, bends tenderly over her baby sleeping peacefully in his cradle by the fire. In the background Joseph, the father, is working at his carpenter's bench. Light shines on a group of cherubs hovering over the baby's cradle. The child is, perhaps, Rembrandt's baby son Titus. Although Mary does not look like Saskia, she may be Rembrandt's idea of a gentle mother who cares for her little child.

HOLY FAMILY WITH ANGELS 1645
Hermitage, Leningrad

Rembrandt etched a portrait of himself as he sat by the window working. He was forty-two years old. His face was lined and heavy. He did not look like the gay cavalier who had once held his lovely bride on his knee. Six years of loneliness had changed him. He no longer wore the plumed hat and velvet coat of a prosperous gentleman. Instead he is dressed in the severe clothes of a Puritan. He does not laugh as he looks at himself in the mirror. The artist's expression is serious as he concentrates on his work; but in his work, Rembrandt had found refuge from his grief.

SELF PORTRAIT 1648
Pierpont Morgan Library, New York

Rembrandt no longer was asked to paint good likenesses of Dutch citizens. Alone in his studio he was free to choose the subjects which appealed to his imagination. In etchings he told stories from the life of Christ. One of the most beautiful is a picture of Christ healing the sick. In the center stands the radiant figure of Jesus. The right half of the picture is dark, but here and there a face or head shines out, and through the deep velvety shadows gradually emerge the forms of those who have come to be cured. The left half of the etching is brightly lighted, and in the light Rembrandt has drawn in outline the figures of the people who have come to see Christ's miracle.

Many times Rembrandt had seen the sad faces of poor sick people on the streets of Amsterdam, and he had sketched their gestures and expressions. Each face in his picture tells a human story of grief, doubt, or hope.

Although no one commissioned Rembrandt to make the etching "Christ Healing the Sick," he sold several prints of the picture during his lifetime. Fifty years after his death, a customer paid one hundred guilder for one of the prints, and from that day people have called Rembrandt's most famous etching "The Hundred Guilder Print."

CHRIST HEALING THE SICK   1650
Pierpont Morgan Library, New York

When the curly-haired Titus was old enough to hold a brush, his father taught him to paint. The little boy learned rapidly and Rembrandt was delighted. Titus spent many happy hours in his father's studio.

One day a pretty young peasant girl with red cheeks and dark eyes came to live in the house on Breedstraat. Titus was now eight years old and no longer needed a nurse. The young girl, whose name was Hendrickje Stoffels, cleaned the house and cooked for Rembrandt and his little son. Quietly she went about her tasks while Rembrandt painted in his studio. Her shy, calm manner appealed to Rembrandt. He liked her fresh simple face, and sometimes he asked her to pose for him. In one portrait her light hair is combed back under a small yellow cap and a white kerchief is drawn demurely around her shoulders. This shy peasant girl, whose dark eyes are modestly lowered, was one of the few loyal friends that Rembrandt ever had.

HENDRICKJE STOFFELS   1650
Collection Sidney J.v.d. Bergh, Wassenaar

Hendrickje always looked tidy and kept the big house neat and clean. Rembrandt, however, cared little for his own appearance. He walked about the city dressed in a spotted smock, which he tied at the waist with an old scarf. A loose beret covered his frizzy hair. The rich gentlemen of Amsterdam hardly recognized the artist who had once been so fashionable. Important citizens ignored him.

Rembrandt's friends were the poor people of the Jewish quarter where he lived. Many of them visited his studio and he used them as models. Their faces appear often in his beautiful etchings of Bible stories.

SELF PORTRAIT   1652
Vienna Gallery, Vienna

Rembrandt's etching "Christ Preaching" is sometimes called "The Little Tomb," either because it once belonged to a Frenchman named de la Tombe, or because, as some people believe, Christ is standing on a platform which looks like a tomb. Around Jesus is gathered a crowd of people who have come to hear him preach. One man with a long thin nose sits, chin in hand, looking thoughtfully into space. Another, with a big white beard, leans forward, listening intently. A woman wearing a white cap sits on the ground, a baby in her arms. Beside her a little boy lies on his stomach and with his finger traces a picture on the ground. Near Jesus stands a stolid figure whose face expresses no interest in Christ's teaching. Some of the people are dressed in strange costumes. One man wears a huge flat beret; and another, the loose trousers, pointed shoes, and striped turban of an oriental.

But Rembrandt was not interested in making a picture of models dressed in costumes. His etching tells a story of real human beings who are listening for the first time to a wonderful message of a great teacher.

CHRIST PREACHING   1652
Pierpont Morgan Library, New York

As Rembrandt's loneliness increased, his understanding of human problems grew deeper. His pictures told moving stories of people who had suffered. Many Dutch artists in Rembrandt's day painted smooth pictures of fruits and flowers reflected in gleaming metal or sparkling glass, but these subjects did not interest Rembrandt. He found inspiration for his pictures in the people he saw in the streets of the city.

One day, however, as he passed a butcher's shop, the brilliant reds and whites of a hanging beef caught his eye. The luminous colors of the heavy carcass seemed to glow in the changing light. Rembrandt painted two pictures of the hanging beef. In one, the woman who peers fearfully from the half-open door of the shop is scarcely visible in the dim background. The great crimson carcass hangs alone in front of the butcher's shop, a masterpiece in pure and vibrant color.

HANGING CARCASS   1655
Louvre, Paris

Plunged in his work, Rembrandt hardly noticed that the rich people of Amsterdam avoided him; but he could not ignore the creditors who came to his door to collect the money he owed them. Although he no longer cared for fine clothes for himself, he loved to fill his house with beautiful paintings and etchings. He spent money recklessly until he became penniless. Hoping to recover his fortune, he borrowed money, but he did not invest it wisely and was unable to pay his debts. In vain creditors clamored for their money. Rembrandt was bankrupt.

These were dark days for Rembrandt, but he still continued to paint great pictures. One of his finest is a portrait of a handsome young man on horseback. He is dressed in a strange eastern uniform, which may have belonged to a Polish regiment. The name of the horseman is unknown, but he is now called "The Polish Rider."

The young man moves courageously through a gloomy landscape of dark forests and perilous rocks. Rembrandt must have thought of the dangerous world through which every man must ride, for it was at this time that he lost his home and all his possessions.

THE POLISH RIDER   1655
©Frick Collection, New York

One summer day in 1656 Rembrandt packed up his canvases, brushes, and a few old clothes. In every room of his big house men were busy making lists of his possessions. Rembrandt was selling his home, his fine paintings, pieces of ancient armor, and precious jewels.

Titus and the faithful Hendrickje followed him to a small hotel in the poor district of Amsterdam. In a bare little room he set up his easel and painted undisturbed. He did not miss his big house and his priceless treasures, which had become a burden to him. When his home was sold he gave the money to Titus.

Titus was fifteen years old when Rembrandt lost his home. He was a handsome young man with blond wavy hair. One day Rembrandt painted his portrait as he sat reading. His sensitive face is bathed in a golden light. His lips are slightly parted and his expression dreamy, as if he is lost in the story he is reading.

TITUS READING   1656
Vienna Gallery, Vienna

Rembrandt painted some of his finest pictures in the bare little tavern room in the slums of Amsterdam. He was often cold and hungry, and his only friends were Titus and the loyal Hendrickje. Because he himself had suffered he understood the suffering of others, and his pictures told of man's grief. External details did not interest him any more. Mysterious landscapes and lofty buildings had disappeared from his paintings. His figures are bathed in an atmosphere of glowing light and deep shadow.

He painted a picture of Saint Peter at the moment when he denies to the servant girl that he is a follower of Christ. A golden light seems to move through the shadowy canvas, picking out the heavy features of the guards in the foreground and lighting up the small room in the background where Jesus is standing. It plays brightly on the figure of the servant girl and finally, in a burst of brilliance, illumines the face of Saint Peter at the very moment that he betrays his master. The beautiful face of the apostle tells a tragic tale of man's indecision and cowardice.

THE DENIAL OF SAINT PETER   1658
Rijksmuseum, Amsterdam

While Rembrandt painted, Titus and Hendrickje worked hard to sell his paintings. One December day in 1660 they opened a small art shop. Rembrandt agreed to paint pictures for the shop in return for a small allowance. His own needs were few —a loaf of bread, a herring, and an occassional bottle of wine. With the money Titus gave him, he bought paintings, fine materials, and pieces of china for the shop. His mind was at peace, for he knew that his son and devoted housekeeper would care for him.

Rembrandt was fifty-seven years old. His eyes were weak after years of looking for hidden light in deep shadow. He could no longer etch fine lines on a copper plate, but his paintings vibrated with life. In ten years he painted fourteen life-size self portraits. When he looked at himself in the mirror he saw a man whose brow was wrinkled, nose bulbous, and eyes puffy, but he did not try to disguise his aging features. He painted his face as he saw it—the face of a man who had suffered deeply.

SELF PORTRAIT   1660
Louvre, Paris

Rembrandt seldom spoke to others of his suffering, but he expressed his sadness in many of his pictures. In his painting of young David playing the harp before King Saul, the old king weeps as he listens to the music and wipes away his tears on the heavy curtain which separates him from David. The young musician, who concentrates on his playing, does not seem to notice the king's grief. Like Rembrandt, Saul suffered alone.

DAVID PLAYING THE HARP BEFORE SAUL   1658
Mauritshuis, The Hague

"The Night Watch" had hung for twenty years in a dark corner of the hall belonging to Captain Banning Cocq's regiment. Few people remembered that the artist who had painted it had once been the most popular portrait painter in Holland. Younger artists who had learned to copy Rembrandt's style were now receiving commissions from Amsterdam's important citizens. But one day in 1662 the director of the clothmakers guild called at Rembrandt's bare little workroom. He wanted the artist to paint a group portrait of the board of directors of his guild. Putting aside his self portraits and pictures of Bible stories, Rembrandt set a fresh canvas on his easel.

He painted a picture of five board members grouped around a table covered with a scarlet cloth. The men are dressed in black robes, broad white collars, and tall black hats. The servant who stands behind the table is hatless. Rembrandt did not try to paint people in action, as he had in "The Night Watch"; nor did he plunge some of them in darkness. The faces of the five businessmen stand out clearly. Although the personality of each is strikingly different, all the members are concentrating on the same problem. The solitary Rembrandt pictured vividly a group of men working together at a common task.

THE BOARD OF THE CLOTHMAKERS GUILD 1662
Rijksmuseum, Amsterdam

One October day in 1662 Hendrickje Stoffels died, and was buried near Saskia in the graveyard of West Church. For fifteen years the modest peasant girl, who could neither read nor write, had been Rembrandt's most faithful helper. She had brought up Titus, made him her business partner, and protected the penniless Rembrandt.

Titus carried on the shop alone. Although he was a talented painter himself, he devoted his time to selling his father's pictures. But in the autumn of 1668, six years after the death of the faithful Hendrickje, Titus died. The shop was closed and Rembrandt again was penniless.

One after the other Rembrandt's friends had left him. He was sixty-three years old and nearly blind, but once again he sat in front of the mirror and painted his portrait. His curly hair had grown white, his cheeks puffy, but his expression was calm. This was the last self portrait he ever painted. He died a few months later.

A lawyer made a list of Rembrandt's possessions—some canvases, a few pieces of clothing, three pocket handkerchiefs, ten caps, and one Bible. No one followed his coffin through the city streets one October day in 1669. The people of Amsterdam did not realize that the penniless artist who was buried in the graveyard of the West Church had left to the world five hundred luminous paintings, two hundred etchings, and nearly two thousand beautiful drawings.

SELF PORTRAIT   1669
Mauritshuis, The Hague

ACKNOWLEDGMENT

I wish to thank Phaidon Press Ltd., London, for giving me permission to reproduce the photograph (Plate opposite page 20) from *The Paintings of Rembrandt,* A. Bredius, Phaidon-Verlag-Vienna, 1936.

BIBLIOGRAPHY

Avermaete, Roger: REMBRANDT ET SON TEMPS. Payot, Paris, 1952.

Benesch, Otto: REMBRANDT'S SELECTED DRAWINGS. Phaidon Press, Ltd., London, New York, Oxford University Press, 1947.

Bolton, Charles Knowles: SASKIA, THE WIFE OF REMBRANDT. Thomas Y. Crowell & Co., New York, 1893.

Borenius, Tancred: REMBRANDT—SELECTED PAINTINGS. Phaidon Press, Ltd., London, 1952.

Bredius, A.: THE PAINTINGS OF REMBRANDT. Phaidon-Verlag, Vienna, 1936.

Brion, Marcel: REMBRANDT. Editions Albin Michel, Paris, 1946.

Chandler, Anna Curtis: TREASURE TRAILS IN ART. Hall, Cushman & Flint, Boston, 1937.

Focillon, Henri: REMBRANDT. Librarie Plon, Paris, 1936.

Goetz, Oswald: THE REMBRANDT BIBLE. The Greystone Press, New York, 1941.

Hind, Arthur M.: A CATALOGUE OF REMBRANDT'S ETCHINGS. Methuen & Co., Ltd., London, 1923.

Hofstede de Groot, C.: DIE HANDZEICHNUNGEN REMBRANDTS. Ervin F. Bohn, Haarlem, 1906.

LaFarge, John: GREAT MASTERS. Doubleday Page & Co., Garden City, New York, 1915.

Ludwig, Emil: THREE TITANS. Modern Age Books, Inc., New York, 1938.

Michel, Emile: REMBRANDT, HIS LIFE, HIS WORK AND HIS TIME. William Heinemann, London, 1894.

Van Dyke, John Charles: THE REMBRANDT DRAWINGS AND ETCHINGS, With initial reassignments to pupils & followers. Charles Scribners Sons, New York, London, 1927.

Van Loon, Hendrik Willem: THE LIFE OF REMBRANDT Van RIJN. Heritage Club, New York, 1939.